The art of growing up

Margaret Kezia Ragland Thomas

BookLeaf Publishing

Presentation by *BookLeaf Publishing*

Web: www.bookleafpub.com

E-mail: info@bookleafpub.com

ISBN: 9789395756730

First edition 2022

DEDICATION

Here's to those who dream,

foolish as they may seem.

PREFACE

A friend of mine gifted me a cute diary for my twenty second birthday and I have this compulsive need to fill a new book with something. Art, tax details, doodles or a quick scribble of a phone number my mum tells me to take down. But instead I wanted to fill it with an assortment of writings that I tend to note down when I follow my train of thought. It's a very personal form of relaxation, almost like I've taken my mind to the mental equiquivalent of a dog park and let it loose to make metaphors and draw comparisons.

It brings me immense joy that I can share this with you and hope that you might resonate with the entirety of what's written or maybe just a phrase. That it makes you forget about time for a second and whisks you away to different worlds.

Being in your early twenties is an odd combination of events and emotions that I often feel my life is a sitcom show with an invisible audience. On days I want it to shine, it rains. When I want to get ahead, the traffic lights turn red. And you just sit there strumming on your steering wheel, impatient to wait and yet scared to move forward.

So these were written from such a viewpoint, of having to let go but being unable to, a sudden perspective of the people you love growing old, the longing of an everlasting love, the excitement of the future and most importantly learning to love yourself as you are.

I truly wish that these make you laugh, reminisce and fill you with an unquenchable thirst for adventure as we navigate the many phases of life.

This is where the fun begins!

Candlesticks

Every year I grow older
I add another candlestick on my cake.
When I was five,
I had five and felt envious about
those who had ten.
I need to live more, I said,
to get more of these twisted columns of wax
that sat like medals of completion.
As a kid, I did not comprehend it's true
significance.
For now I know, the more you get,
the less time you have
and I pondered about it
when I lit up forty six candlesticks
for my mum, when I joined her party at twenty
four.
It felt melancholic, the toss of time
suddenly too real, pulling me apart.
But I was reminded about
my five year old self,
I now have more candlesticks since then,
I have seen more of life since then,
But to get to forty six, I need more.

I need to live more, I said again.
So live, I shall.

Twisted columns of wax

Sunsets are green

I love all things green
from funky umbrellas to trees
but mostly, I love the way
the colour soothes me in the mid of May
and I know the world is technicolor
blooming around me like a field of flowers
but ever since that day in December,
I love all things green.

A cold winter's day,
almost near Christmas day,
I was sitting alone in a park bench,
rather blue, missing spring's scent
but then he sat next to me,
my heart, began to buzz like a bee.

Now the sun began to set, you see
and in a world of white,
it was only him and me
with his long woolen coat
and I'm in my head afloat.
He turned to me with a pleasing smile
and I caught sight of his eyes.
I forgot that the sky turned orange,
for to me, they were green.

from funky umbrellas

I love all things green
to trees.

Polkadot Avenue

You wear a shirt, like that of a ladybird
and it dances to the ways of the wind
It's a summertime candy eyed crush
that I believe will pass by and
get carried away by drifting clouds.
Buttoned down, only halfway
and I tell myself it will pass by,
It's half truth and a blatant lie.

Cause when you lay next to me,
I want to walk my fingers down
Polkadot Avenue,
between the crevice in your chest
and set the buttons free,
pull back your coolers to see,
If you're suave like me.

Cause you're sunshine and I've got a darkside
I told myself, love was not for me
but why do you have to go and
make it look easy?
I'm a tempest in awe of a ladybird.

Cause my life has never been easy,
for you're a whimsical make believe,

making me believe that things could be different,
if I lean into you gentle hands, breezy smile and
lemonade words.

I want to bury my little secrets
and mermaid tears
in your Polkadot Avenue as you hold me up
I've never felt this from someone else,
this comfort.
Just you and me and Polkadot Avenue.

It's a summertime candy eyed crush,
it won't pass by, it's a brush with love
and I'll stay,
I'll stay for you.

you wear a shirt,

like that of a ladybird.

Time Traveller

I'm seated in front of him
but I'm not here entirely
rather I'm miles away
No, planets away
existing in timelines
all in my mind
Falling in love
over and over
with someone new
someone who's made up of pieces of you
and I'm there
and I'm here
listening to him talk
I'm trying to get up and walk
to leave it all behind.
For he thinks I need a bit of fixing
but he would only waste his years.
Being a time traveller, is who I'm meant to be.
Suspending time on what ifs
and traversing alternate planes
Do I do it to fix the past?
Perhaps in the hopes of a new future?
Or is it to relive the same feeling
over and over?
I do not know.

What I do know is,
I'm hardly here
I'm always there
and elsewhere
Just me and my little time machine.

time machine
Just me and my little

Voids

I've always been drawn to voids,
empty spaces that could be filled
with art or stars or words,
like your heart, that I want to touch
and bring forth the sweetest spring
to take up all the walls in your mansion
with poems and portraits and letters.
Give me all your scars and I'll paint over them
murals of new beginnings and memories.
If only you could hold
my pigment smeared hands,
you might see yourself the way I see you.
So open up and hand over your emptiness
and I'll patch it over with my finest fabric,
for when you catch the light this time,
you will be one of a kind,
like the northern lights.
If you're worried you're a blank canvas,
don't fret,
for my fingers are itching to block you in,
find every crevice, turn every stone,
to mark out the extent of your universe.
For if you give me your entirety,
it's only a matter of time,
like a candle illuminating a dark room,
you will be devoid of voids.

give me all your scars

and I'll paint over them

Parallel Universes

We exist in two universes.
One that is real and
One that we want to be true
and these two versions of ourselves
never interact.
But they commune together in our mind,
One speaking of things as they are,
the other speaking of things as they could be
and neither believes the other
but for a brief period
in our mundane existence
we catch a glimpse of the other,
in a dusty window pane as you
walk down the street,
when the rain has wet the pavements
and your reflection matches your stride
or when you sit at home, with no one around,
that old mirror calls for you.
To see yourself,
The what is and the what could be.
The what was and the what has become.
It's all in there, fighting
to come to the surface.
The power to choose,
in the hands of a version

that is the most indecisive of creatures
and as hypocritical as ever
you do believe,
for a second or in a dream,
that maybe the version in your head
and the version you're living
might merge into one.

THE WHAT WAS AND THE WHAT HAS BECOME

THE WHAT IS AND THE WHAT COULD BE

The wolf and the tiger

I find it fascinating that I am
drawn to the wolf and the tiger,
two halves of myself,
the moon and the sun.
The wolf known for its loneliness
and the tiger for its elusiveness,
both of which I practice daily.
Lonely like paw prints on fresh snow.
Elusive like a glimmer of orange
among the green.
They don't have to say much
and neither do I,
you can look into our eyes and know
that we've seen things you may never know.
I never appear to those that try their best to find
me.
I appear,
suddenly like a silver silhouette
amidst the dark trees
or slowly in a sleeping jungle
to drink from the crystal lake.
I appear,
to the nymphs and to the ones
who have drawn me up in their minds.
I roam free like the wind,

so if you have a house upon the hill,
you might only see me thrice.
For I tend to go where my heart leads me.
I'm fire and ice,
I'll cool your burns and warm your hands
but if you ever wish to entrap me,
you will become frozen ash.
For I am the wolf and the tiger,
The sun and the moon,
I'll only come home,
if my heart belongs to you.

Elusive, like a glimmer of orange among the green

Lighthouse keeper

A lighthouse keeper, bent over the rail,
looking out to the waves
as the light swivels and scopes the sea,
for any ships headed her way.
She's been here for decades,
listening to the cicadas sing
till the moonlight bleeda blue.
The world, a puzzle of silhouettes
and the only light behind her.
There's a hum in the air,
a feeling of anticipation.
That one day, the house on top of the hill
might cast a golden glow
and she won't be cold anymore.
So she waits,
for a merman to wash up shore,
a lonely sailor to come back home
or for someone who had been
searching for her.
But for now, it's only her and the lighthouse,
beaming a light on the horizon,
sending a signal out to the world.
That she's here,
that one day she would look out
to the dark waters,

to see a tiny boat coming towards her.
Until then, she's the lighthouse keeper,
tending to the bulbs and keeping a tally
of the days, storms and rainbows,
because one day,
the lighthouse will stand alone,
but she won't.

The house on top of the hill
will cast a golden glow

so she waits,

Pretty Pony

I yearn to run wild and free,
the feeling of fresh grass beneath my feet.
I am well capable to be on my own,
but you don't think so.
And in the pretext of security and luxury
you trap me in the lasso of your necessity.
I used to watch blue mountain sunsets
but now I'm put behind a fence.
No proof of ownership, but I'm yours
because you say so.

"Pony, braid your hair and tuck in your hooves."
"Pretty Pony, if you love me, win this battle for
me."
"Pretty little pony, won't you jump this hoop for
my friends?"

I used to eat raw honey and drink glacier waters
but now I'm fed sodden oats, twice at best
and everytime I bite against the bit,
I get the whip.
I never needed a saviour, but you deemed
yourself so,
for you like to marvel
at butterflies in a glass jar,

while telling the world
you saved them from hawks.

"Stupid horse, run faster."
"How dare you disobey your master?"
"Crazy animal, I should have
never given you a home."

But you won't throw me away, never leave me to
god's way,
cause if not a destrier, I could still be a sumpter.
You say other horses have it worser,
that for me you've given the world,

What use is the world?
If it was never mine to begin with.

Won't you jump this hoop for my friends?

Wings of Fire

We know the story, how it goes,
a hundred million times
Daedulus made wings, for him and his son.
One wanted to escape,
while one wanted to fly.
I never romanticized it,
maybe because I was a girl,
I felt it was never written for me.
We watch as Icarus flies close to the sun,
with wings given to him and it ruins him.
Now for what these men did,
it was "Fly, but beware the sun.", for the boys
and "Never fly and waste your wings.",
for the girls.

I played a stand-in Icarus in a school play
in fifth grade,
where I spent the whole night making my own
wings.
Out of glue and recycled newspaper,
but when I wore them for the first time
I knew in an instant, I would never done
what Icarus did.
For to me, to even have wings was forbidden.
But my marvelled creation soon saw it's end,

my bullies tore it to shreds.
I held the paper pieces in my hand but
let the knife twist in my heart.

I would have never flown close to the sun
in an attempt to touch it,
because it burns within me.
My true wings differed to what these men built,
it was not made with wax and feathers
but rather with blood, bone and tears.
Wings of fire don't melt away,
they stay hidden,
with the spark of rebellion.
"Don't fly and waste your wings."
For you a scared I might take over the expanse
of your sky.

They do it for power, songs of glory and
monumental statues.
While I need to do it for my survival, freedom
and right.
Icarus and I are not the same, our lives have
been different for years.
And for the sake of lore I could never waste
my wings of fire,
for what if I fly higher than the sun.

Wings of fire don't melt away

Truce

When do you call for a truce?
When can you seize this war?
between your mind and your heart,
your body and soul,
the past and the future.
For when you were a child
the world was black and white
but now you stand on a vantage point
to see it is gray
and they say be glad in the present,
live in the now,
But how?
When you battle yourself daily
against what you want and what is given.
This need to shine a light on your talents,
to find your hidden self,
that you wake
knowing you are meant for more
but not knowing where you fit in.
Why am I not satisfied?
Is that what all dreamers are cursed with?
The need for a better world
but not knowing how to create it.
And it's a crutch,
when you walk about,

creating worlds in your head
only to be in one that doesn't cater to you.
There's a war outside,
There's a war within,
and in both cases
you wave a white flag
in the hopes for a treaty and a truce
so you can finally get on to living.

when can you seize this war?

How do you love?

How do you love?
When people do not want to be read.
I roam the aisles of a forbidden library
where the books shy away from having
their pages from being looked at,
where their stories are erased and rewritten
just so I might not be able to decipher
it's true meaning.
But then, there exists another kind,
the one with pretty covers and empty pages,
ones that throw themselves from the shelves
and land into your hands, their stories
lost to time, crafted to suit everyone,
losing their originality,
it's language slack and lacking flair
and I'm a reader looking for something real,
a story that would mend my heart,
a red string bookmark to tie together my broken
pieces
and words that would ease my pain
that I can recite them over and over.
So I ask
How do you love?
When no one truly wants to be loved.
When no one truly wants to be seen.

The only one who craves this
is the one who roams the aisles.

I'm a reader looking

for something real

Running

When I'm running,
the world stops, my worries fade.
I'm like a wolf chasing it's prey,
the wind rustling against me
giving the pleasure of feeling
I'm finally getting somewhere,
that in a dreamscape
I've picked up my mess and trudged past
the point where I had broken down.
A milestone,
and so I run a mile.
It grounds me, the rhythm of my feet
and the need to never look back.
There's only one goal, to move,
to get ahead,
this need to achieve,
finally gets accomplished.
So running,
running helps me,
whether it's away from my fears
or towards my next dream,
I'm always running.

THERE'S ONLY ONE GOAL, TO MOVE, TO GET AHEAD

You chose me first

I find it beautiful that you chose to
love me even before I was a cell.
When I existed in the dark,
before my sinews were knit together,
that you were there
when I drew my first breath,
as I waddled around and grew up
to play in the mud and ride bicycles.
You sat next to me as the world got harsher
telling me that I'm beautiful
cause you made me so.
That even though I retreat to the dark,
you always find me.
As I sit alone in the train
looking out the window,
you paint the skies just for me
and when I question, struggle, fight
You're my coach,
in my corner of the boxing ring
backing me up, teaching me to fly
and when the voices in my head
tell me I'm too complicated, to intense
to ever be able to witness love
you gently remind me,
wiping away my tears,
that you chose me first.

you paint the skies just for me

The corporate woman

She says she never cries,
her slicked back hair probably tells you why.
She's perfect in everything she does,
everything that requires
a game plan or strategy.
Her fingers wage war using a keyboard,
her voice, formidable on the phone.
Winged eyeliner so sharp,
it could cut you right down to your bone.

The click of her heels against the pavement,
she lives on a timeline
with no time for anyone else,
that as long as she keeps her heart in a clinic
she'll never fall sick
and the only gray she'll ever know
was the suit she owned.

But in the rare moments she looks away
from her demanding phone and clingy laptop,
she watches the one thing
her strategies and logic
could never help her with,
that her reservations
were always only for one

and her mind utterly alone.

But her hair's slicked back,
her gray armour bolted tight,
her life, a video tile
with a blurred background.
She survives, she'll thrive later.
So she never cries,
tears take up time on her timeline.
She's ruthless and intense
"All she ever wants is success."
So she never cries,
as she sips tea in her balcony,
her home phone long dead,
her hair let loose, ready for bed.

She never cries,
was the only consistent lie
she could ever uphold
and the hidden truth,
only her pillow covers know.

She lives on a timeline

with no time for anyone else

Aftermath

People say you never forget your first love,
but what I can't forget is the aftermath.
I spent everyday learning his secrets,
he was a pirate surrounded
by his band of thieves
and I was the girl who dreamt of the sea.
So I would dance around my living room,
wearing an eye patch and a wooden sword
but the more I got close,
I got to know that he only saw me
as his next pillaging venture.
In his greed, he wanted
to break open my shell,
to get to the red beating jewel.
I was just another golden goose.
The pain of my broken hull would result in silent
tears,
and the fear of love, cause it was a hoax.
It didnt matter, when the eartquake happened,
but it was the years it took,
to build back my home,
to paint over the words he spoke,
for in my naiveity to impress him,
I believed them.
I soaked him in, standing in the

corner of the room,
to create a version of him in my head
and memorized the tone of his cologne.
The aftermath.
It's not as worse as before,
I see the cracks and remember
that now I'm stronger
but I would walk down the street,
someone would pass by me
with same perfume he wore
and I would need a minute,
for long ago I wanted it
to be the incense of my life
but now,
its a pungent smell of a lingering memory.
So the aftermath,
I deal with it daily
but now I own my own ship,
ready to set sail across the seas.

BORING
CRAZY
MEAN
SELFISH
To paint over the words you spoke
To build back my home,

Scented erasers

I didn't know much about life,
how could I, I was hardly two and a half.
When all the kids were told to sit still,
you answered all my questions and
let me dream big dreams.

I didn't know the weight of duty I would face,
early on in my life
and how that would
diminish the days of my past but I could
never forget the days
I spent in the sun with you.

I didn't know how fast time was,
for only yesterday you were waiting for me
outside my class to buy scented erasers
for fifty paise
and take me back home safe and sound.
I didn't know those moments
would pass us by.

Like when you ran with me
without a care in 'Poochi' park
or when you took the bus with me on
my first day of school.

I felt special cause my Aachi was cooler than
anyone else I knew.

I didn't know what it meant,
when they said you were getting old,
but now I do.
Now I guide you through hallways,
just the way you once did.
For if it wasn't for you, I would not have a
childhood to look back to.

I don't know much about life,
how could I, compared to you
I'm only twenty two,
but I now know what to make of it,
for you carved out a legacy from nothing,
teaching me that life could be beautiful
in all it's stages.

I don't if you know,
even though I may not show it,
is that I think about you often, always grateful
that you graced my life with your presence
because everytime I pass by scented erasers
in the grocery aisle,
I'll remember you.
Everytime I ride the bus,
I'll remember you.
Whenever I smell lavender,

I'll remember you.

I'll remember you.

Only yesterday you were waiting for me outside my class to buy scented erasers for fifty paise

Fingerprints

I'm an old book, all my pages
smothered with your fingerprints.
A mark that you've been everywhere.
A sign that you've seen everything
and yet you come back to re-read.

You take me to the garden
to tape together my torn pages
that for every word that is written on my skin
you erase them with your lips.
Being known was all I ever wanted,
but you've given me something
I never imagined.
You traversed my soul and hold me close
tucking away my hair like a bookmark thread.

You take me everywhere,
your fingertips, a perfect fit
around the grooves of my spine,
my words on post it notes, you place them
in any space you find.
To the ones who never discovered me,
you brag and hail their missed opportunity.

As the candle light fades

and the moon wanes,
your hands continue to hold onto me
with such esteem, with such care
that now I can't belong to someone else.
All my words have been taken up by you
and in my empty pages, are pictures of you.

all my words have been

taken up by you.

Playground

No more riding our bikes through the streets
in mid-afternoon heat with
no shoes on our feet.
No more throwing our bags on the couch
and relishing the fact there's no school
for a month.

Now we're all part of the rat race
in some form or shape.
So would it be fine if I knock on your door
and say,

Meet me at the playground
when then sun touches down.
Can we share a laugh and keep company
in these lonely swings and merry go round.
Now everything I do is through a screen
so won't you come out and play?
I don't want a friend request
instead shake my hand and
help me build sand castles in the sand.

No more lazy evenings watching looney tunes
then call your best pal to behave like bufoons
No more skipping out on classes

and homework
to search for tadpoles, only to muck about in the
dirt.

Between then and today we grew up
Now all we do is feel left out.
So would it be ok to knock on your door
and say,

Meet me at the playground.

MEET ME AT THE PLAYGROUND

A list of my favorite things

The sound of birds singing in the morning.
Crisp cold air that makes the blanket feel like a
warm hug.
Watching the foam form over my tea as I stir
through it.
Walk down the street as sunlight filters through
the leaves.
The five minutes I wait at a bus stop.
A golden sun setting over meadows.
Warm water running over your feet and blood
rushing to your toes.
The sound of someone's laugh.
A blue sky and fluffy clouds.
A musician playing a song in a busy street.
When you kick of your boots and remove
your socks.
The rumble of thunder and flash of lightning.
Closing the door after the last guest leaves.
Opening the door when my post arrives.
The chime of an old clock.
The smell of an old book.
The calm before a storm.
A familiar song.
Summer welcoming me with a sweet breeze.
Salt air and the glistening sea.

Misty gardens and tall trees.
The smell of coffee and ink pens.
Paint smudged fingers.
The ping of a message .
Anything to do with Christmas
and
you, all of you.

birds singing in the morning

G. David

I told you about a dream
and you said I should write a book.
You searched for greatness from
the confines of your little dusty room.

I saw you through the eyes of a child
but the world saw you differently.
You were the lone cowboy with a brutal past
who walked the edge of town.

You wore your smile like
a Jazz age gentleman,
hiding away your green eyes
behind aviator glasses,
driving through the streets
in your shiny white car,
searching for some form of acceptance.

You were never angry with me
like a beast who had befriended a pixie.
Teaching me to cheat on board games
and that I could be anyone I wanted to be.

Now your house sits alone without it's charm
cause you're not there,

sitting in the corner browsing recipes
or to see me chase dreams and graduate.

I buried a part of myself with you,
a golden glimmer memory of
driving around in your scooter
to buy glitter pens
without having to worry about school.

And yet you live on, in my mind,
in the faces of my father and brother
and the voice in my head that says
I could be anyone I wanted to be.

I see you in dreams, from time to time,
anytime I read a story or hold a book.
You were many things but to me
you were a proud English professor
who taught me,
I could be anyone I wanted to be.

I told you about a dream.

you said I should write a book.

What is your favourite memory?

ACKNOWLEDGEMENT

To have the courage to come forth and share my writings, I want to start of my thanking Bookleaf publishing for giving me an opportunity to share my work.

My parents for always backing me up when I shared my dreams and for having faith in me. My brother, everytime I try to talk myself out of it, he's there to remind me to go after what I want.

A couple of the most amazing friends I've been blessed with. Ekshaw, my really cool travel enthusiast friend (who is also an amazing photographer), thank you for always telling me to dream bigger and for being a kindred spirit. Rajagopal, he's cooler than Batman, thank you for being there at every pivotal point of my life and for being my best friend. Kishore, thank you for your long phone calls and for your amazing jokes, they mean the world to me. Kiah, my awesome singer songwriter bestie, thank you for being in my corner and supporting me. Love you all so much!!

Finally, JC. I don't think I would be here without you and everyday I'm grateful you're in my life.